This Room Is a Mess!

Written by Anne Patterson

Illustrated by Pamela R. Levy

"Magda!" said Amado. "This room is a mess! You cannot wait. You need to clean it before Mom gets home."

Magda made a face. "I hate to clean!" she said. "Will you help me?"

"No," said Amado. "I am baking a cake. But I know you can do a good job. And when your room is clean, you can have a slice of cake."

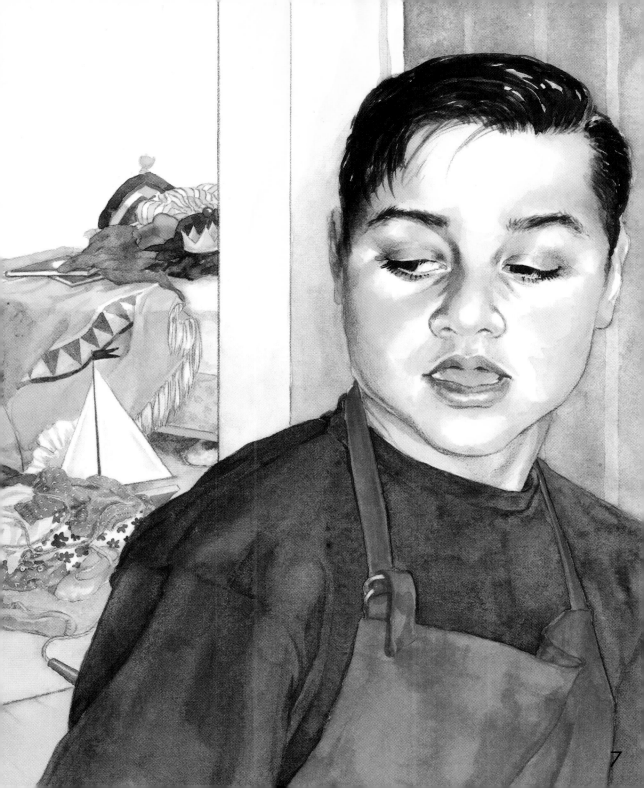

Magda frowned. She picked up
two jump ropes and put them in a pile.
She picked up five socks and put them
in another pile. She picked up one boat
and three hats and nine trucks.

9

"Amado," said Magda. "My room is clean. May I have a slice of cake?"
"Let's go see," said Amado.

"Magda, you did clean your floor," said Amado. "But look at your bed! These things need to be put away. You know the rules. I know you can do a good job before Mom gets home."

13

Magda tried again. She threw the socks in her closet. She threw the jump ropes and the trucks on top of them. Then she threw in the hats and the boat. She pulled up her sheet and blue blanket.

15

"Amado, my room is all clean," said Magda. "May I have a slice of cake?"

"Let's go see," said Amado.

"Oh, Magda," said Amado. "You did clean off your bed. But look at your closet! These things need to be put away. Try one more time. I know you can do a good job before Mom gets home."

Magda tried one more time. She picked up the boat and the jump ropes and the trucks and put them in the toy box. She put the socks in her hamper. She put the hats on the top shelf of the closet.

"Amado!" called Magda. "My room is clean!"

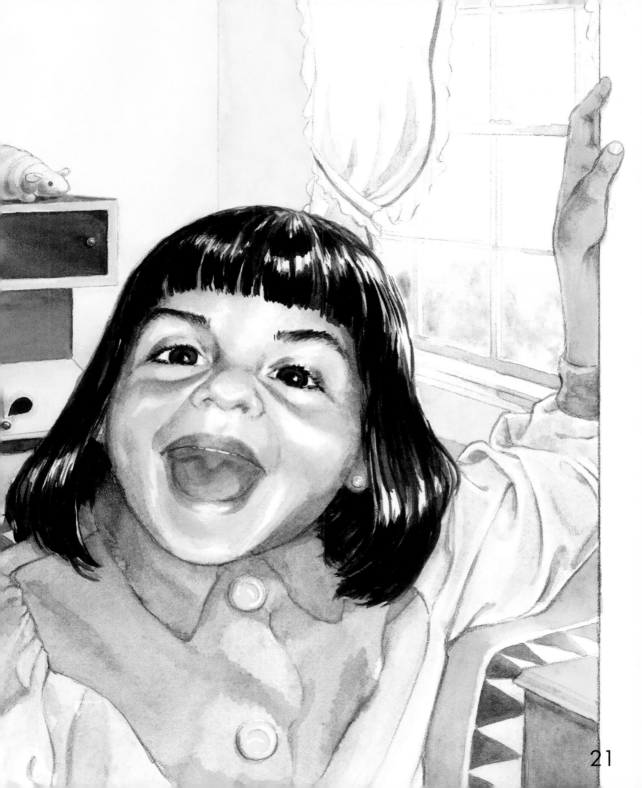

21

"Magda, you did it!" said Amado. "I knew you could do a good job. Mom will be happy, too. Come have a slice of cake."

"Amado," said Magda. "This room is a mess! You need to clean it before Mom gets home!"